Congratulations and best wishes

To

From

Graduation

Marie D. Jones is widely published in both books and magazines and has contributed to titles that include *The Silver Book of Hope* and *Bless This Marriage.*

Jan Goldberg has written 32 books and over 400 articles. Her work includes contributions to three other titles in this series: *Sisters, Friends,* and *Grandmother.*

Picture credits:

FPG International: Jeff Baker; Walter Bibikow; Richard Brown; Gary Buss; Ron Chapple; Peter Gridley; Alan Kearney; Eric Pearle; Barry Rosenthal; Mark Scott; Carl Vanderschuit; VCG; Wides & Holl; John Wilkes; **SuperStock:** The Grand Design, Leeds, England; Private Collection/Christian Pierre; Peter Sickles.

Let the world be your campus,
creating new opportunities with
the lessons you have learned.

Wonder...is the root of knowledge.

ABRAHAM JOSHUA HESCHEL

Graduations are like recipes.

They provide one of the main ingredients

For your ultimate success!

As you turn to face your future, know that
all you have learned in the past will be your rudder,
guiding your boat across the vast sea of potential
to the distant shore where destiny awaits.

True success in life finds you only when you
successfully learn to be yourself.

*T*each others what you have learned,
share the lessons of your life experience,
give freely from the storehouse of knowledge within,
and your life will have worth and meaning.

$\mathcal{I}$f you truly open your heart

To new opportunities,

You will see

That the possibilities

Are endless.

So look to your future

With the excitement and joy

It truly deserves.

Photo

Education is an ornament in prosperity
and a refuge in adversity.

ARISTOTLE

If you keep taking steps that move you forward, you will always be heading in the right direction.

It is the appreciation of beauty and truth, the striving for knowledge, which makes life worth living.

MORRIS RAPHAEL COHEN

Hold fast to your dreams as you climb the heights of
success. Let no challenge or obstacle deter you
from the destiny that calls to your soul.
This is your time to fly; the endless sky is your domain.

Education is a treasure.

PETRONIUS

Education can be learned, knowledge can be acquired,
but wisdom must be experienced.

Life begins with baby steps.

Education allows you to take giant leaps.

There are no leaps too far;

No jumps too wide;

No lifts too high;

Set your sights on the stars!

The direction in which education starts a man
will determine his future in life.

Plato

There is more to education than getting good grades and wearing a cap and gown. Education teaches us the magic and power of learning and instills in our hearts the never-ending desire to grow, to expand, and to become more than we were before.

Be proud, for you have achieved a great thing.

Be grateful, for you have overcome all obstacles.

Be generous, for you have been given the
   gift of knowledge.

Be enthused, for you hold the key to the life
   of your imaginings.

You have studied hard and learned much.
You have accomplished a lofty goal. Now take
a moment to bask in the joyful glow of
achievement. You deserve this day in the sun.

Photo

*L*ove of learning is a pleasant and
universal bond, since it deals with what
one *is* and not what one *has*.

FREYDA STARK

$\mathcal{L}$et all that you have learned serve you well as you pursue new dreams and goals. Let all that you have achieved be a solid foundation upon which you can build a bright future.

$\mathcal{I}$f a man empties his purse into his head no one can take it away from him. An investment in knowledge always pays the best interest.

BENJAMIN FRANKLIN

Keep hold of instruction; do not let go;

guard her, for she is your life. PROVERBS 4:13

There are many words of wisdom
friends and teachers will impart,
but the wisest words of all will come
from deep within your heart.
So follow not the road well toiled,
nor walk another's way,
but find the path that's yours alone
and boldly seize each day.

$\mathcal{S}$tep into the future with your eyes clearly
focused on your dreams.

$\mathcal{A}$s long as you live, keep learning how to live.

SENECA

$\mathscr{A}$pply the same passion, purpose, and power
to your dreams as you have to your education, and
nothing will be impossible for you to achieve.

*R*emember that the future
holds limitless possibilities for all
who believe in themselves.

*A*lways extend your arms a little farther
than you can reach.

Photo

Today marks the
celebration of an end
to all the hard work
you have done and the
anticipation of a whole
new path now
unfolding before you.

The greatest achievements of your life begin the moment
you take the wisdom and knowledge you have gained
and go out into the world to share it with others.

Determine your life's path.

Then compose a road map

To aid you along the way.

Keep it clearly visible at all times

So that you can stay on course

And ultimately arrive at your destination.

When the door behind you closes, ahead of you will be a window to a whole new world of opportunity.

*L*et not your education end here. Be a beacon of hope for others struggling to reach the place you proudly stand in today. For you now hold the power to motivate, to inspire, to encourage. No longer the student, you become the teacher.

You are the captain of your ship, the navigator of your destiny.
Let your education guide you to greater seas of success and
accomplishment as you set sail for the far horizon of your dreams.

*E*ducation is the gift that keeps on giving.
Long after those school days have ended,
the effects of knowledge continue to multiply, expand,
and empower every aspect of your life.

$\mathcal{S}$et a standard for yourself that
gives you the incentive to
increase your abilities,
stretch your capacities,
and widen your imagination.

A good education is like having an inner well
that supplies your life with limitless opportunities.
The more you continue to learn, the deeper the well gets,
and the greater those opportunities become.

Education is a legacy we leave to others.

$\mathcal{I}$ have learned...that if one advances confidently in the direction of his dreams, and endeavors to live the life which he has imagined, he will meet with a success unexpected in common hours.

HENRY DAVID THOREAU

*G*raduation is a promotion in the career that is your life. Continue to strive for excellence, and you will one day be your own boss, working toward the goals and dreams of your own envisioning.

May you never
stop learning as you
leave the halls of
academia. May you
never stop achieving
in the greatest
school of all—the
school of life.

What sculpture is
to a block of marble,
education is to an
human soul.

JOSEPH ADDISON

You stand at the edge of tomorrow, facing the chasm that separates where you have been from where you want to be. With education, enthusiasm, and experience to propel you, take the giant leap of faith and set down firmly upon the solid ground of your future.

With wisdom and knowledge to guide you,
let this day be a whole new start to live
the life you've dreamed of.

Photo

Find the light that makes you
shine and then use those rays
to illuminate your way.

*T*here is no greater
opportunity to learn than to
move out into the world and
apply the skills and
knowledge you have
accumulated to the
challenges of everyday life.

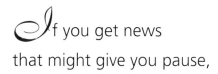

*I*f you get news
that might give you pause,

just know that there is
something better for you
waiting in the wings!

Always be willing to push yourself in
new and different directions.
You could end up at a worthy
destination you never even dreamed of!

The ultimate aim of the human mind, in all its efforts, is to become acquainted with Truth.

ELIZA FARNHAM

Stand for something,
and your life will have purpose.
Give of yourself,
and your work will have meaning.
For anyone can get an education,
but not everyone can share that knowledge
for the betterment of all humanity.

Only the educated are free.

EPICTETUS

Education is the potter's wheel
upon which the hands of
knowledge and experience
mold and shape invisible potential
into visible opportunity.

The end of learning is the
formation of character.

KAIBARA EKKEN